Horse
Coloring Book
For Adults

An Adult Coloring Book of 40
Horses in a Variety
of Styles and Patterns

ISBN-13: 978-1519798824
ISBN-10: 1519798822

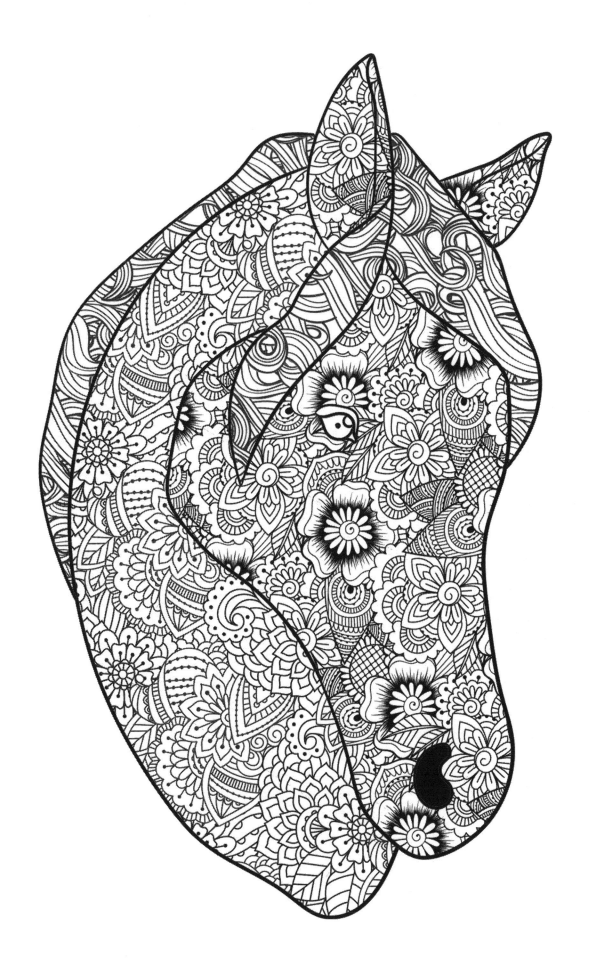

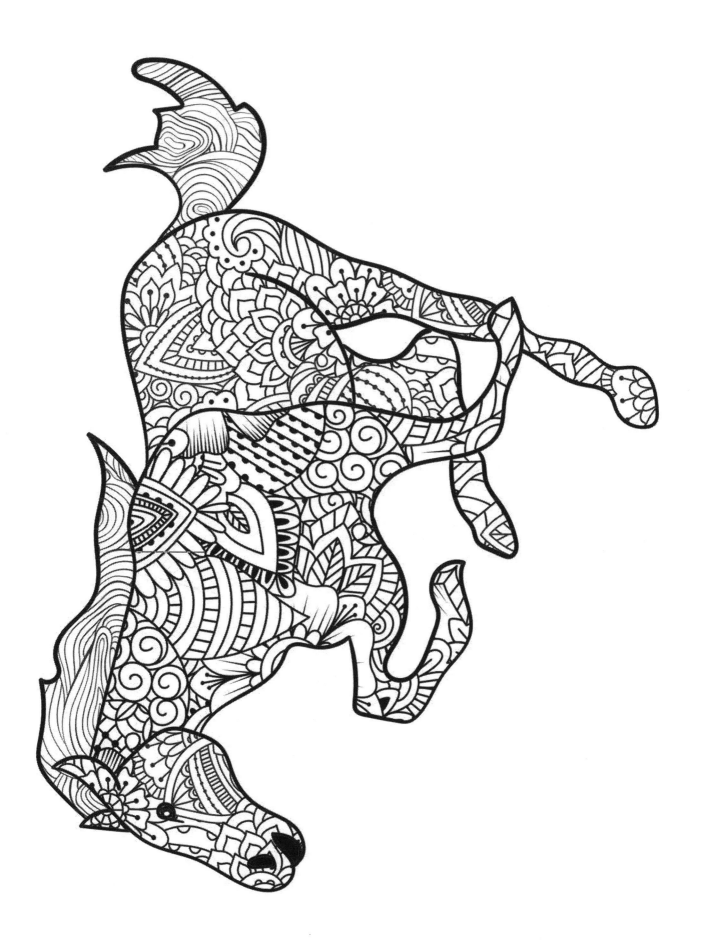

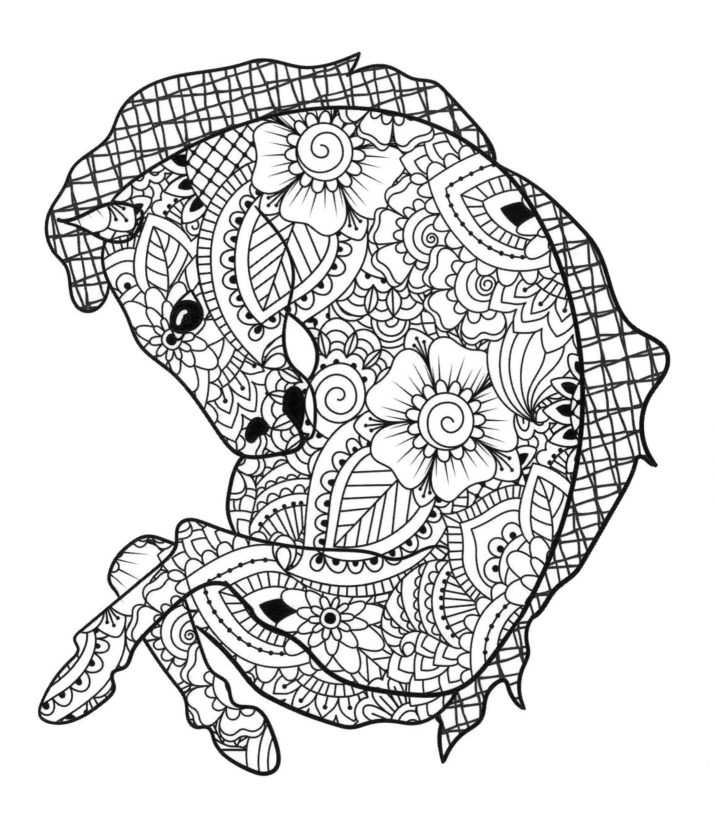

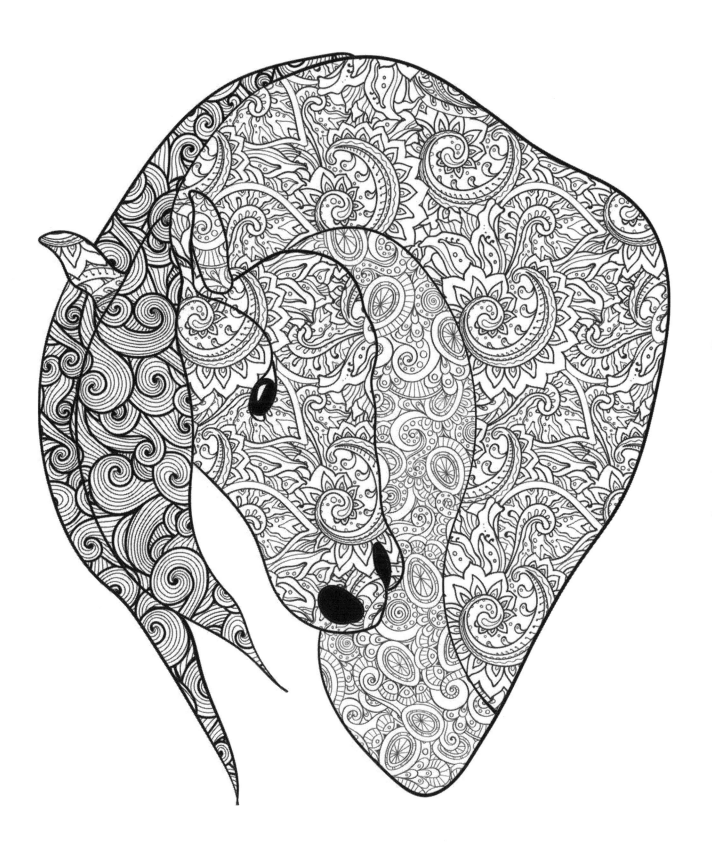

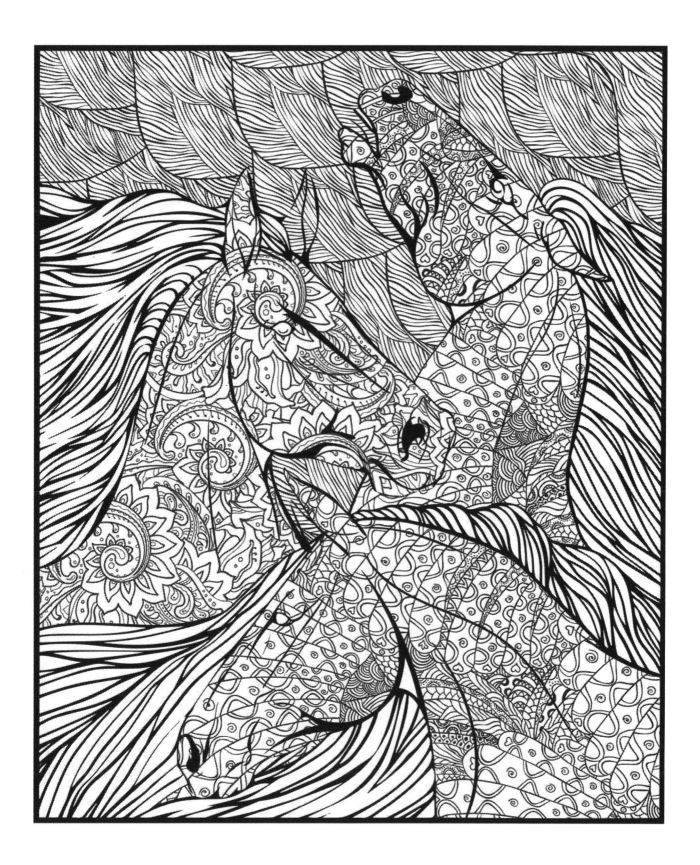

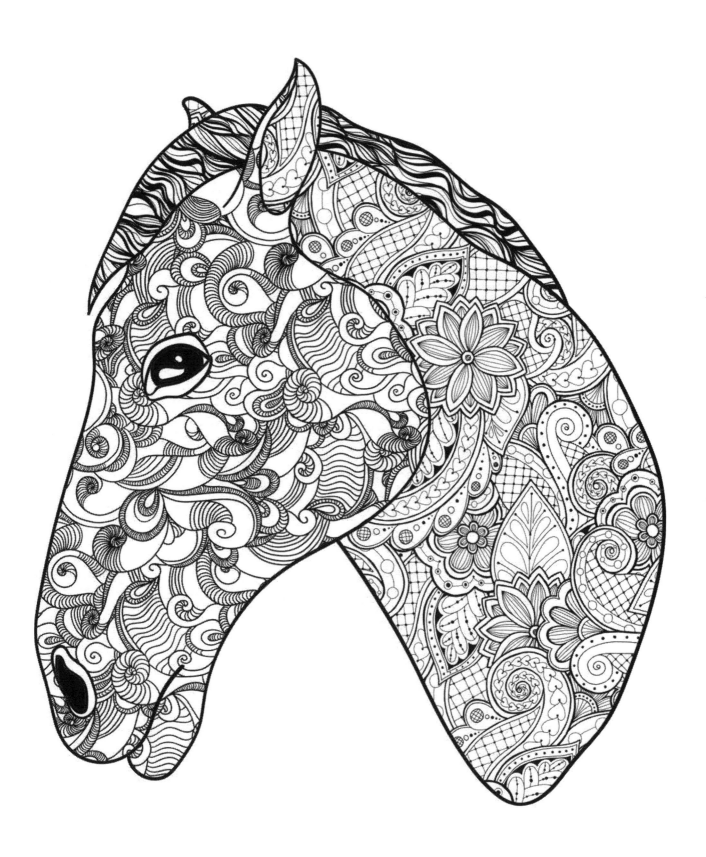

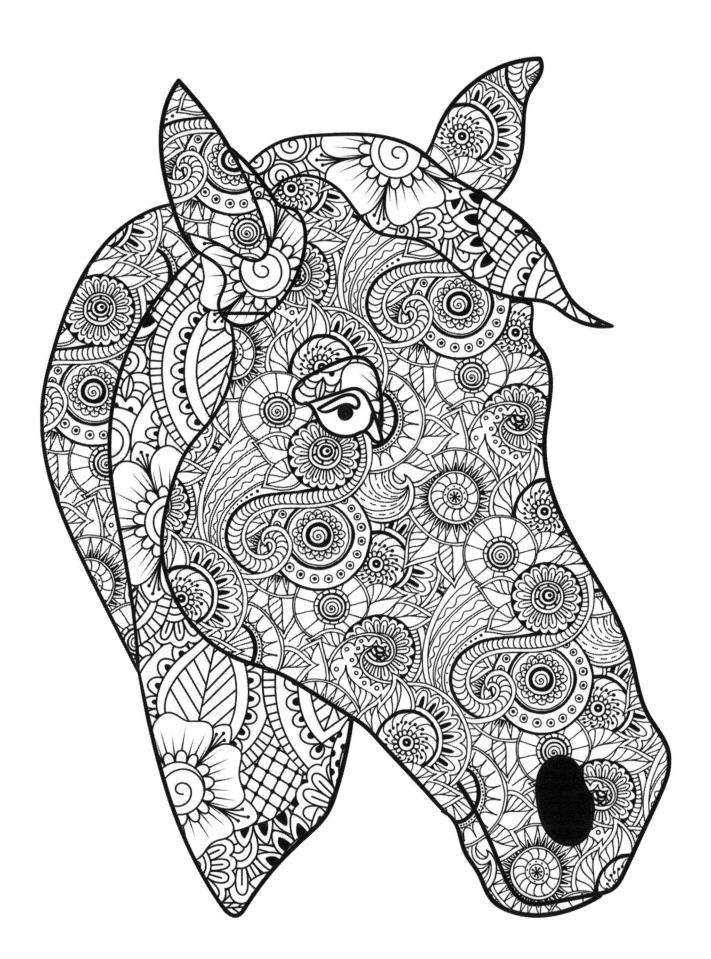

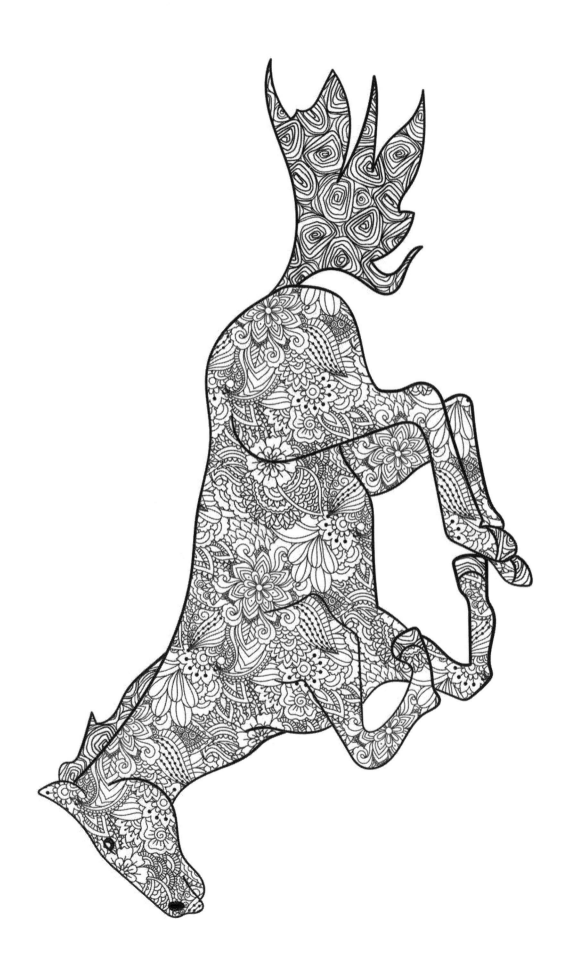

37359510R00047

Made in the USA
Middletown, DE
29 November 2016